KID'S KEYBOARD COURSE BOOK #2

MW01139514

Contents

HAL•LEONARD® CORPORATION
7777 W. BLUEMOUND RD. P.O. BOX 13819 MILWAUKEE, WI 53213

WELL, HERE WE GO AGAIN. WE HAD A LOT OF FUN ALREADY, DIDN'T
WE?...BUT THAT WAS JUST THE BEGINNING. IN THIS BOOK, YOU'LL START
BY LEARNING ABOUT PLAYING ON THE BLACK KEYS. OF COURSE, WE'LL
PLAY SOME REALLY GREAT SONGS TOO.... SONGS LIKE "OLD MACDONALD
HAD A FARM," "POP GOES THE WEASEL" AND "GREENSLEEVES."

WE'VE MADE ONE CHANGE IN THIS BOOK.... THERE ARE NO COLOR BARS
ABOVE THE NOTES IN THE SONGS. YOU PLAY SO WELL THAT YOU DON'T
NEED THEM ANY MORE.

AS BEFORE, BE SURE TO HAVE YOUR OWNER'S MANUAL NEAR BY IN CASE
YOU NEED TO FIND OUT SOMETHING ABOUT YOUR KEYBOARD. YOU MIGHT
ALSO WANT TO KEEP THE REGISTRATION GUIDE HANDY... THAT'S IN BOOK I,
REMEMBER?

OKAY...LET'S GET GOING!

Sharps ♯

In BOOK 1, you played songs using only the white keys. In the song BAA! BAA! BLACK SHEEP, you will play a note called F-sharp (or F♯). A sharp sign (♯) in front of a note almost always means that you should play a black key. When this happens, the name of the note changes a bit, for example — from F to F-Sharp. F-Sharp, your first black key, is shown in the diagram below.

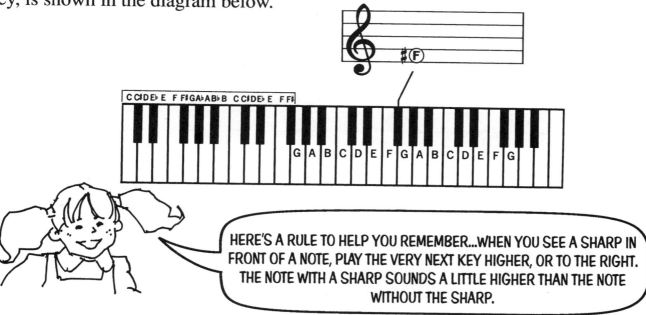

HERE'S A RULE TO HELP YOU REMEMBER...WHEN YOU SEE A SHARP IN FRONT OF A NOTE, PLAY THE VERY NEXT KEY HIGHER, OR TO THE RIGHT. THE NOTE WITH A SHARP SOUNDS A LITTLE HIGHER THAN THE NOTE WITHOUT THE SHARP.

Getting Sharper!

HERE ARE TWO SHORT EXAMPLES FOR YOU TO PLAY THAT USE F-SHARP. YOU'LL FIND THEM EASIER IF YOU USE THE FINGER NUMBERS SHOWN.

New Chords: D , A7

Be sure to locate the right keys for these chords before you play the song.

Baa! Baa! Black Sheep

Registration 2
Rhythm: Rock or 8 Beat

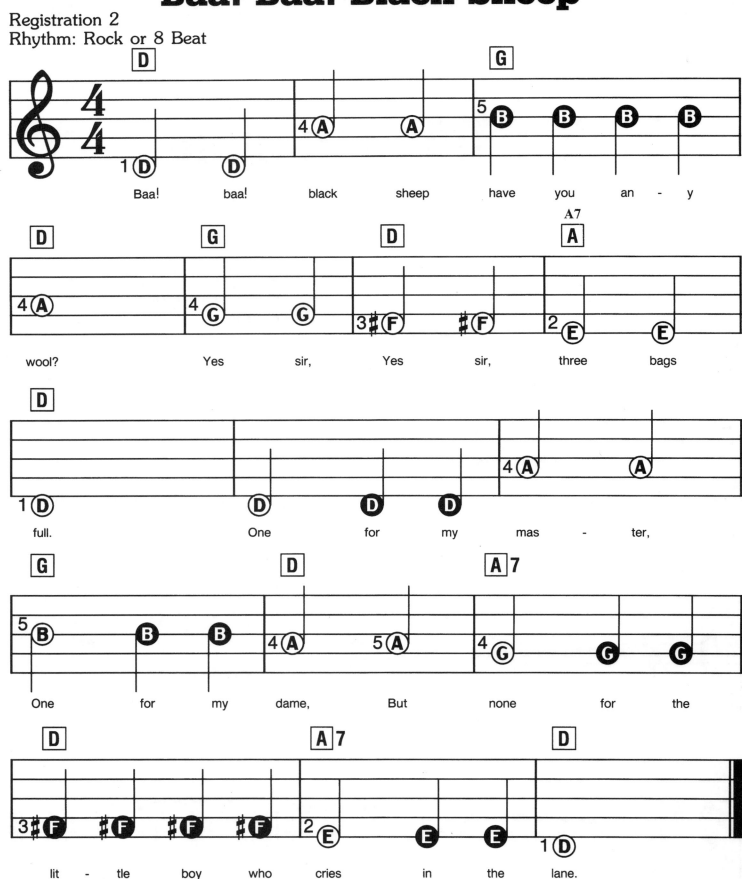

New Note: High D

In your next song, ON TOP OF OLD SMOKY, you will play a new note, high D. Here is what it looks like and where it is on your keyboard.

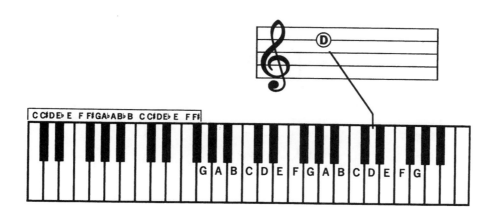

Fingering

Look at the finger numbers in ON TOP OF OLD SMOKY very carefully and follow them exactly as you play the song. The finger numbers will help you along and will make sure you don't run out of fingers along the way!

On Top Of Old Smoky

Registration 1
Rhythm: Waltz

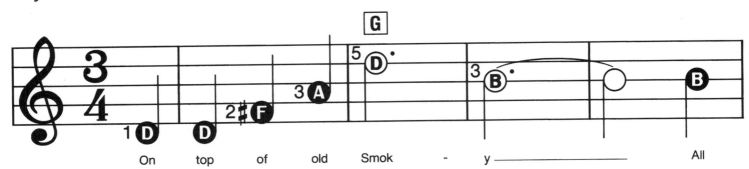

On top of old Smok - y _____ All

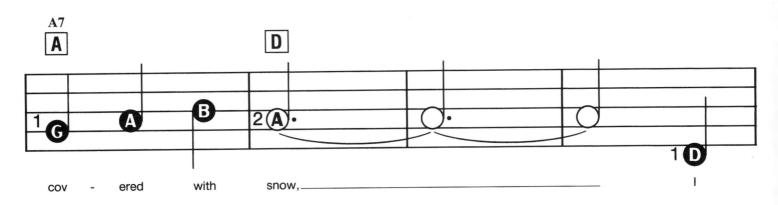

cov - ered with snow, _____ I

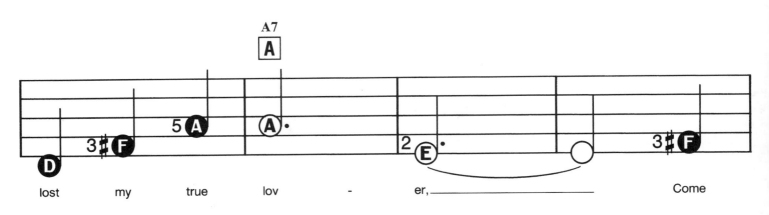

lost my true lov - er, _____ Come

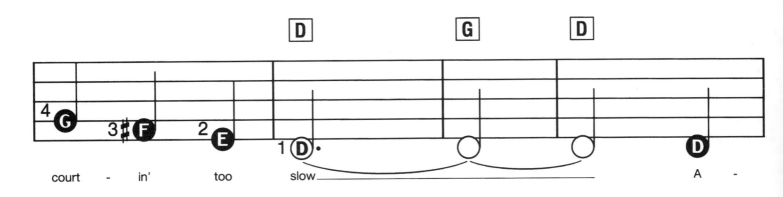

court - in' too slow _____ A -

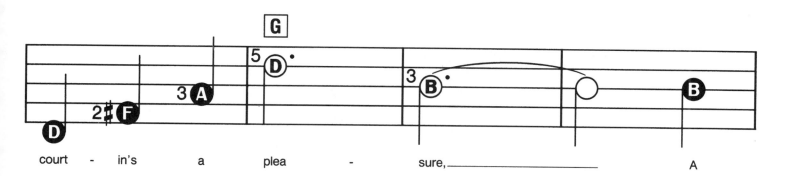

court - in's a plea - sure, _____ A

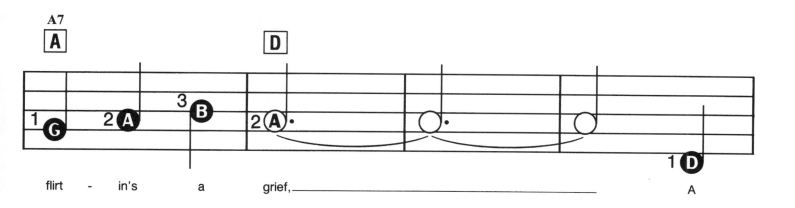

flirt - in's a grief, _____ A

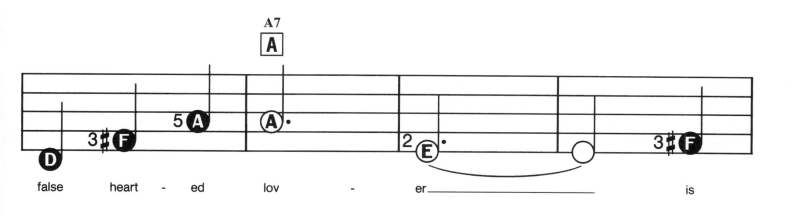

false heart - ed lov - er _____ is

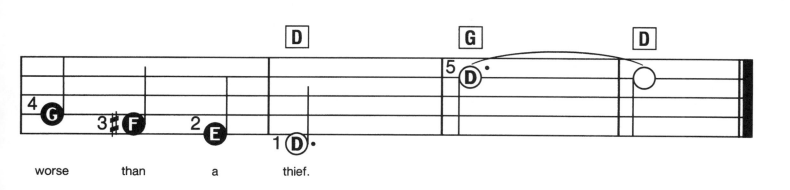

worse than a thief.

New Note: High E

POP! GOES THE WEASEL uses a new note, a high E. It is one white key higher than the high D you just played in ON TOP OF OLD SMOKY. Here's what your new high E looks like and where it is on your keyboard.

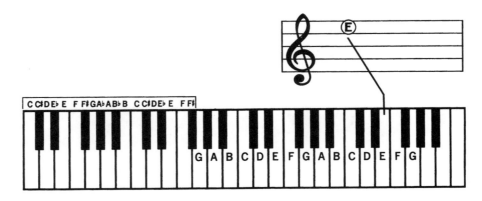

Pop! Goes The Weasel

Registration 5
Rhythm: Waltz

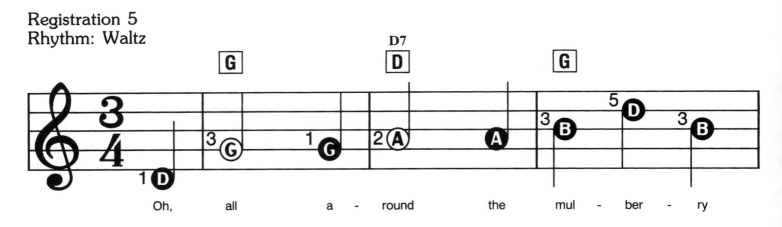

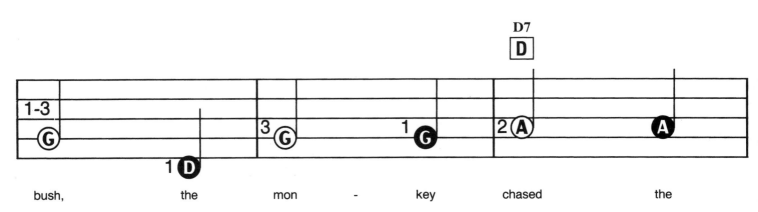

wea - sel. The mon - key

thought 'twas all _____ in fun.

Pop! goes the wea - sel.

Brahms' Lullaby

Registration 8
Rhythm: Waltz

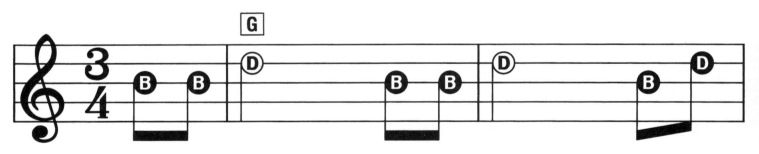

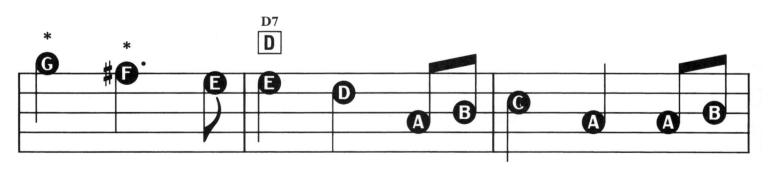

* These are two new notes, high G and high F-sharp.

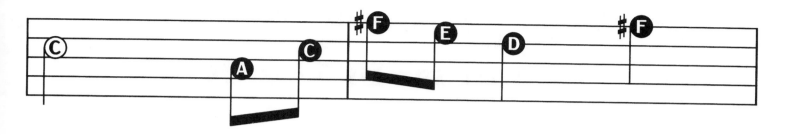

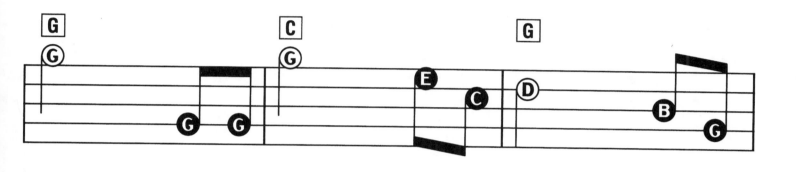

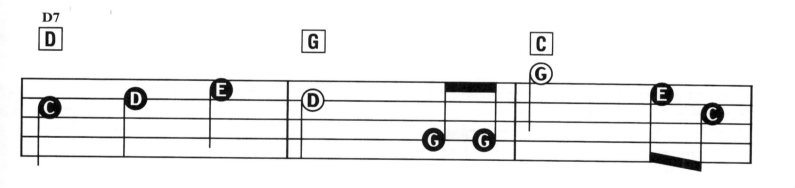

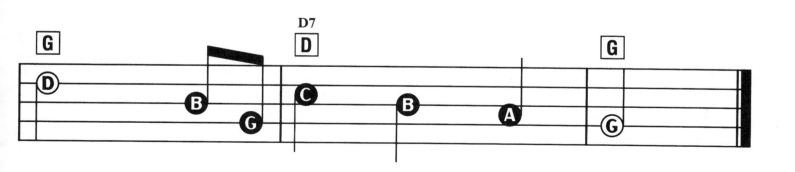

More Sharps

There are no chords in this song so you can practice playing only the melody. When you can do it smoothly, try adding the built-in drums if you wish.

The Farmer In The Dell

Registration 3
Rhythm: Waltz

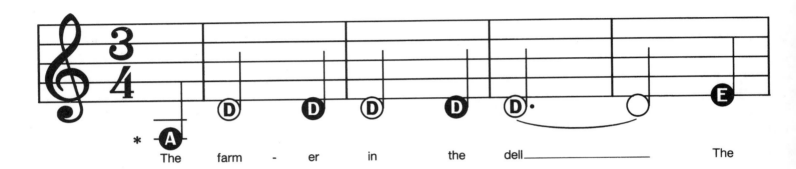

The farm - er in the dell_____ The

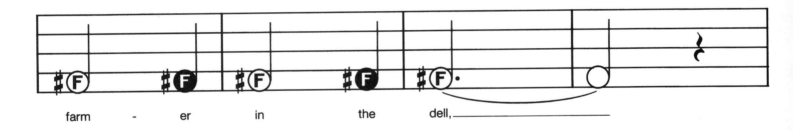

farm - er in the dell,_____

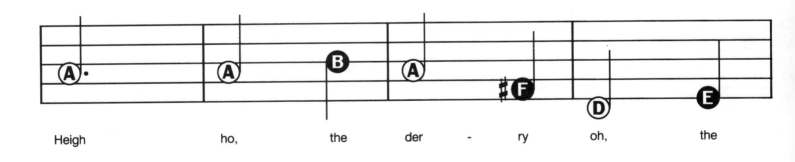

Heigh ho, the der - ry oh, the

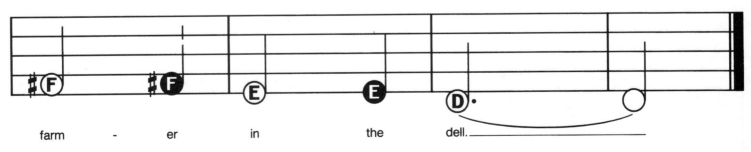

farm - er in the dell._____

* This is a new note, Low A.

Flats ♭

In your next three songs, you will play a B note with a flat (♭) in front of it. A flat sign in front of a note almost always means that you should play a black key. As with sharps, the flat is added to the name of the note.

Here is where the B♭ note is on the keyboard.

Let's B Flat!

Down In The Valley

Registration 8
Rhythm: Waltz

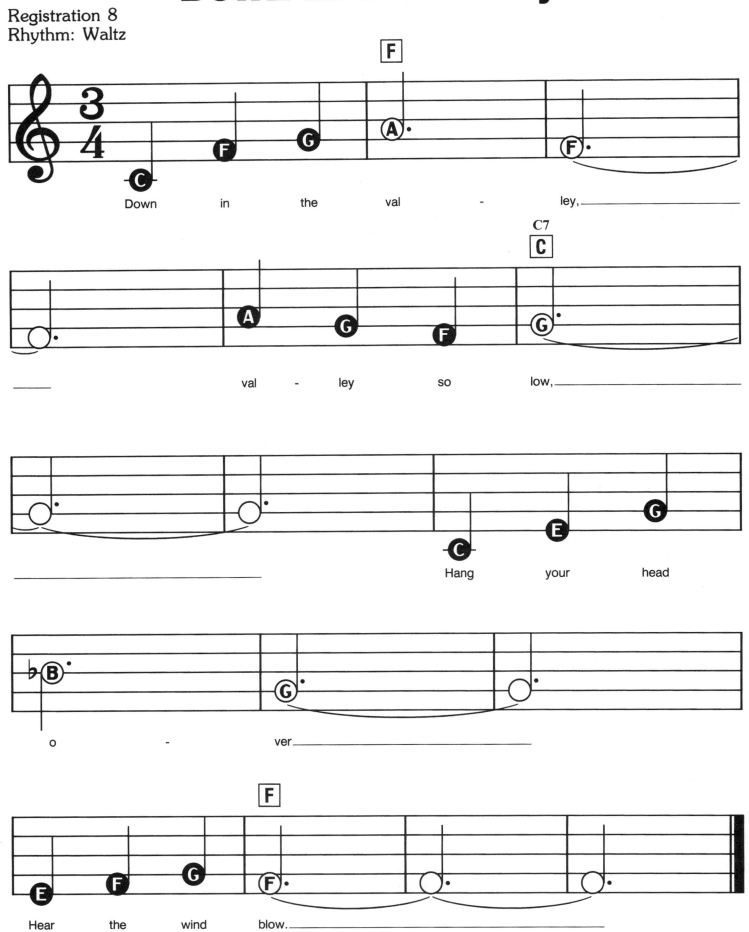

Down   in   the   val - ley,   val - ley   so   low,

Hang   your   head

o - ver

Hear   the   wind   blow.

Oh Where, Oh Where Has My Little Dog Gone

Registration 5
Rhythm: Waltz

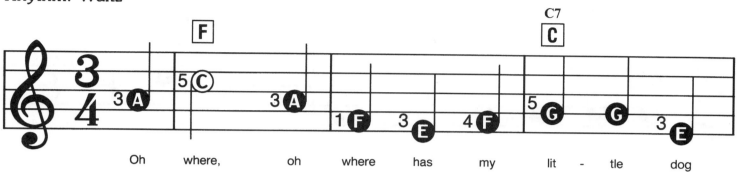

Oh where, oh where has my lit - tle dog

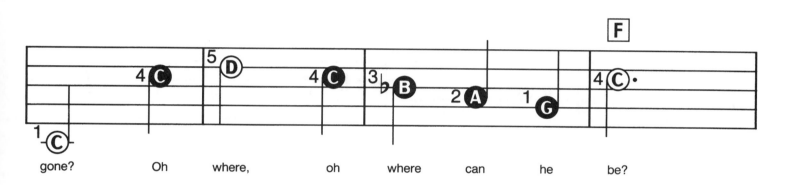

gone? Oh where, oh where can he be?

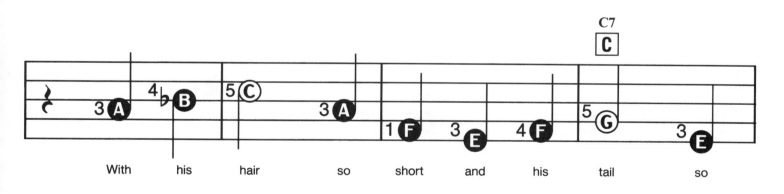

With his hair so short and his tail so

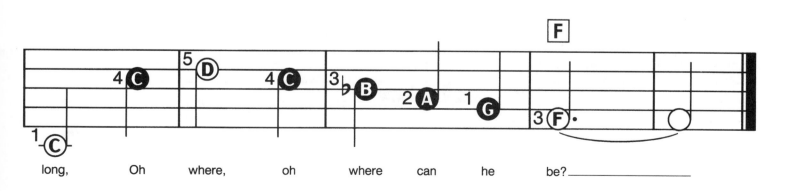

long, Oh where, oh where can he be?_____

Looby Loo

Registration 2
Rhythm: Waltz

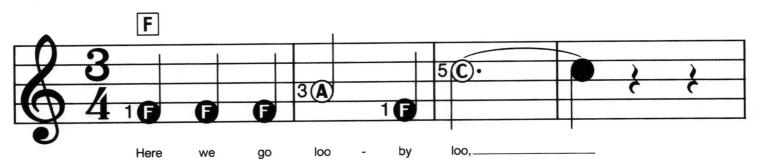

Here we go loo - by loo,

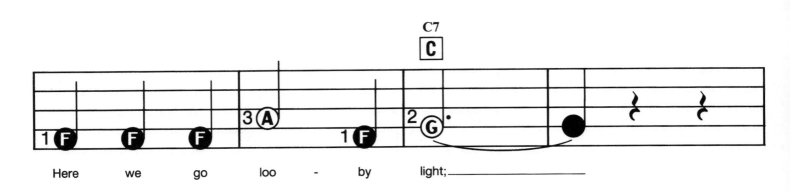

Here we go loo - by light;

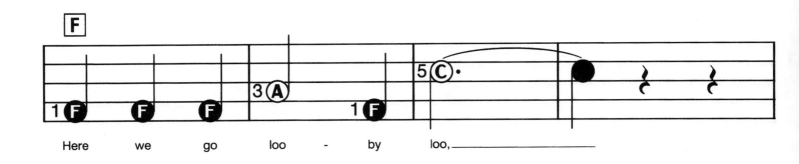

Here we go loo - by loo,

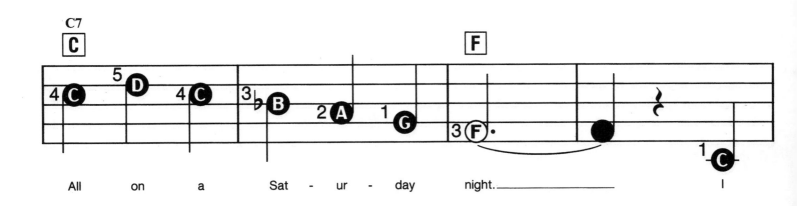

All on a Sat - ur - day night.

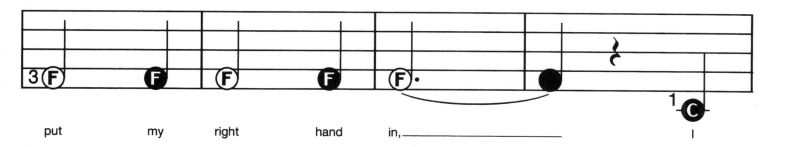

put   my   right   hand   in, _____   I

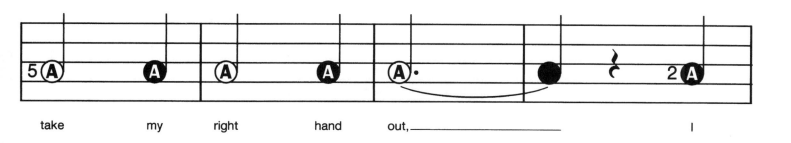

take   my   right   hand   out, _____   I

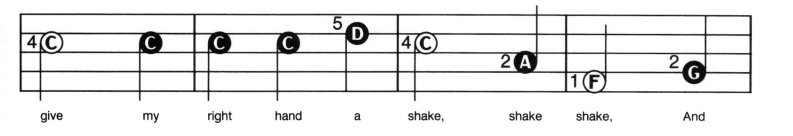

give   my   right   hand   a   shake,   shake   shake,   And

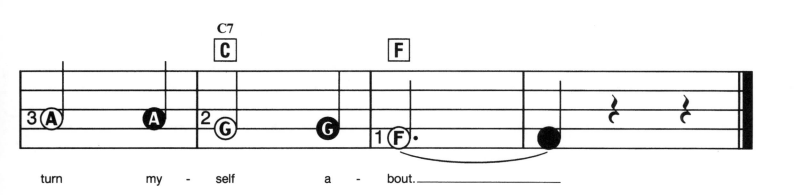

turn   my   -   self   a   -   bout. _____

New Chord: B♭

Here is the B-flat chord on your keyboard. You will use it in OH! SUSANNA.

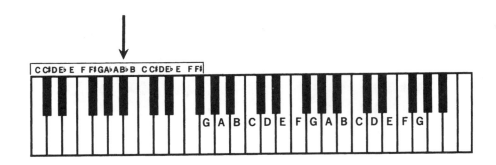

Oh! Susanna

Registration 3
Rhythm: March

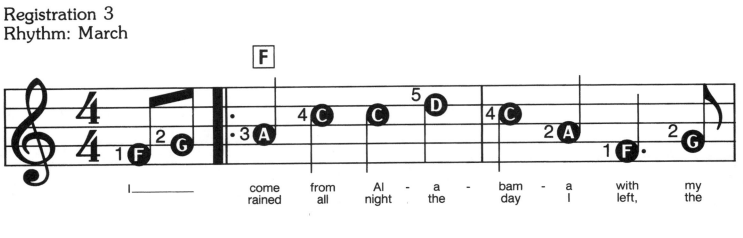

| | come | from | Al | - a | - bam | - a | with | my |
| I | rained | all | night | the | day | I | left, | the |

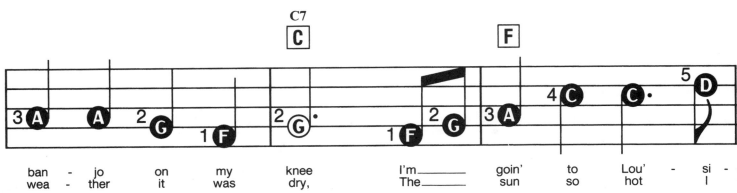

| ban | - jo | on | my | knee | I'm | goin' | to | Lou' | - si | - |
| wea | - ther | it | was | dry, | The | sun | so | hot | I | |

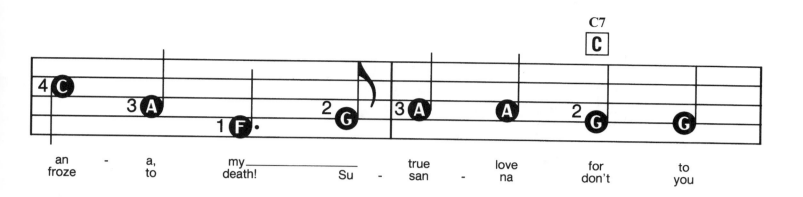

an   a,   my   true   love   for   to

froze   to   death!   Su   -   san   -   na   don't   you

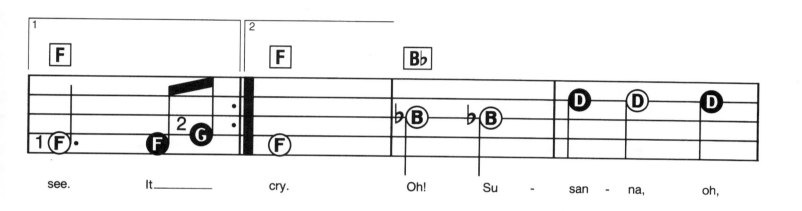

see.   It   cry.   Oh!   Su -   san -   na,   oh,

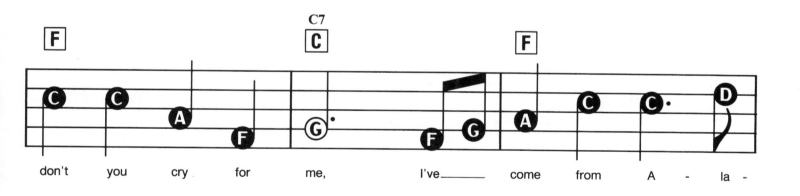

don't   you   cry   for   me,   I've   come   from   A -   la -

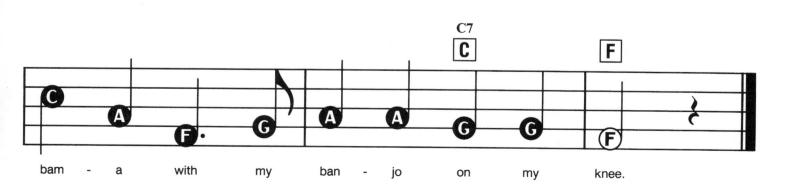

bam -   a   with   my   ban -   jo   on   my   knee.

Getting Flatter

She'll Be Comin'
'Round The Mountain

Registration 7
Rhythm: March or Polka

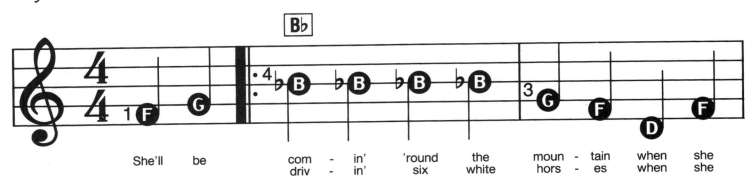

She'll be com - in' 'round the moun - tain when she
driv - in' six white hors - es when when she

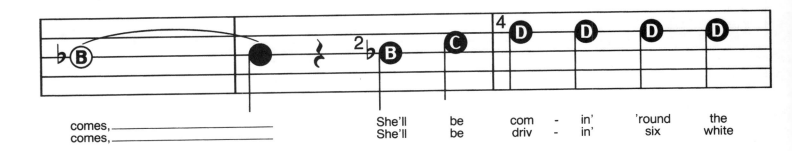

comes,_____
comes,_____

She'll be com - in' 'round the
She'll be driv - in' six white

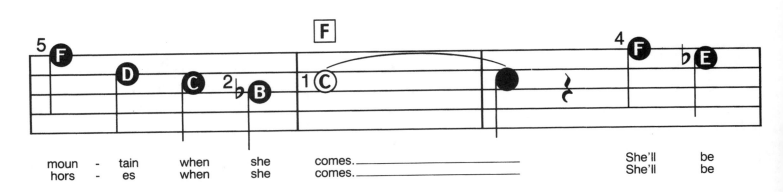

moun - tain when she comes._____ She'll be
hors - es when when she comes._____ She'll be

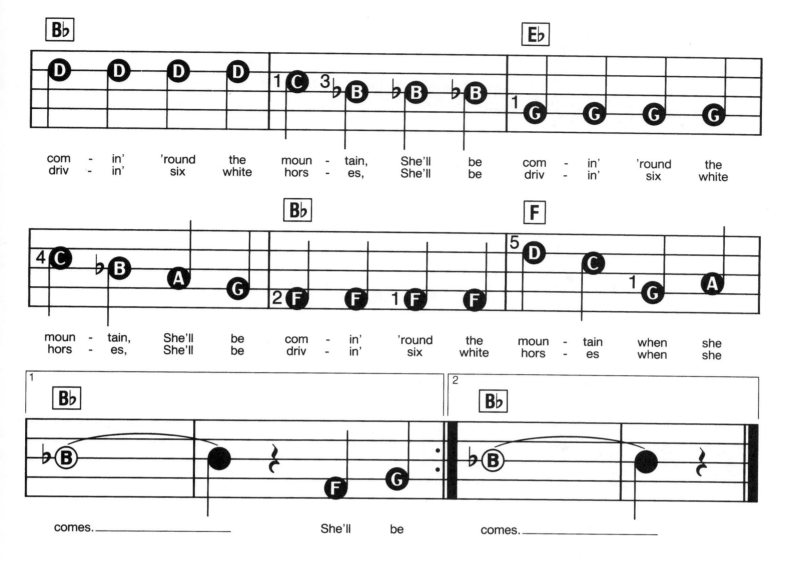

com - in' 'round the moun - tain, She'll be com - in' 'round the
driv - in' six white hors - es, She'll be driv - in' six white

moun - tain, She'll be com - in' 'round the moun - tain when she
hors - es, She'll be driv - in' six white hors - es when when she

comes. _____ She'll be comes. _____

Black Keys Have Two Names

The picture below shows you the sharp and flat names for all of the black keys.

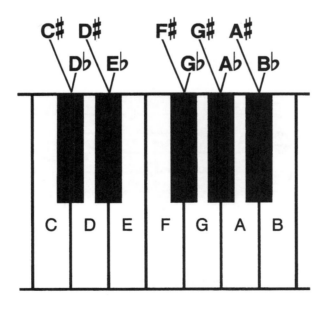

Don't let this worry or confuse you. Actually, every key on your keyboard, black AND white, can have two names. There are a number of reasons for this but none of them have anything to do with playing well or having fun learning songs.

Leaps And Fingerings

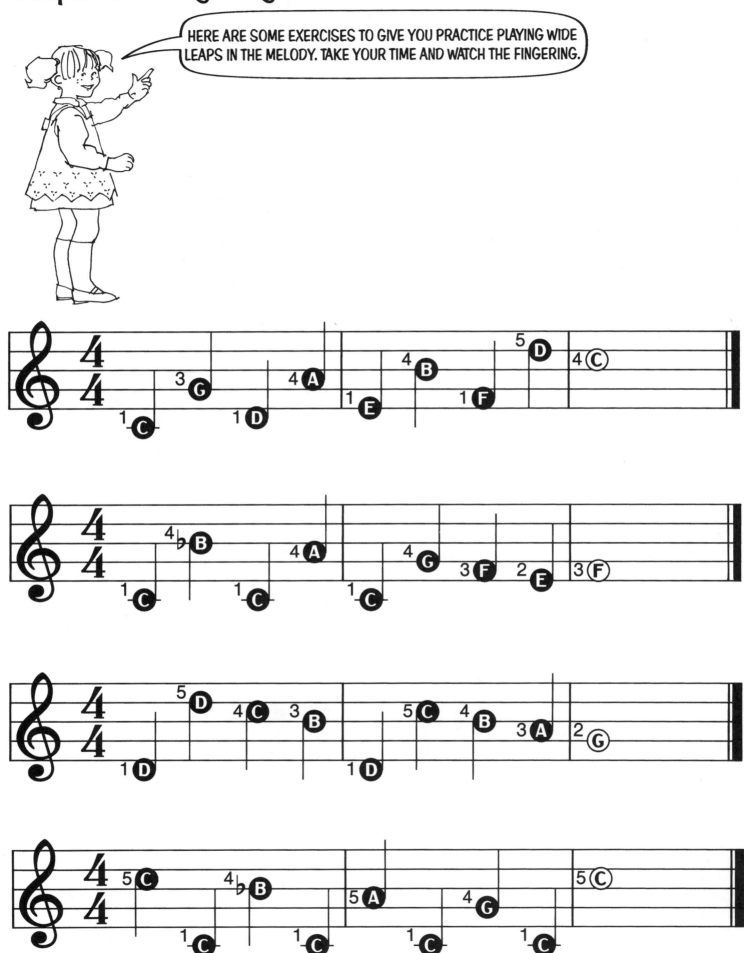

Minor Chords

HERE'S ANOTHER NEW SUBJECT, THE MINOR CHORD. "AMAZING GRACE" USES AN E MINOR CHORD. IN THE MUSIC, THE CHORD SYMBOL IS Em. LIKE SEVENTH CHORDS, MINOR CHORDS USUALLY NEED TO HAVE MORE THAN ONE KEY PLAYED. CHECK YOUR OWNER'S MANUAL.

Amazing Grace

Registration 2
Rhythm: Waltz

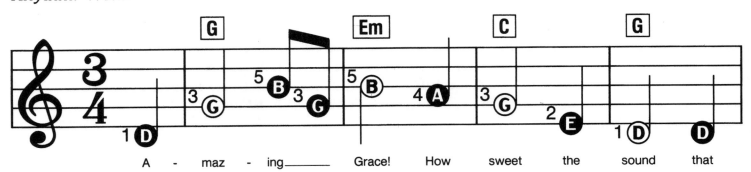

A - maz - ing Grace! How sweet the sound that

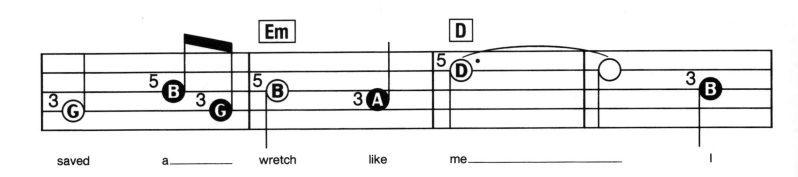

saved a wretch like me I

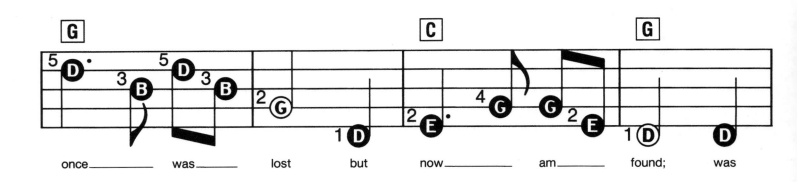

once was lost but now am found; was

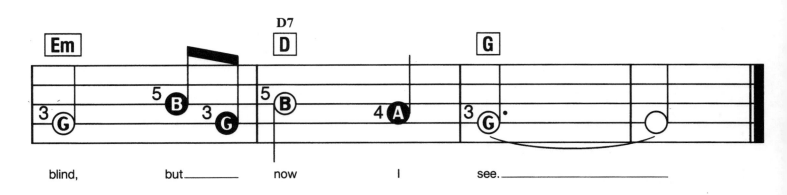

blind, but now I see.

Making Changes As You Play

Changing voices and rhythms while you play can make your music more fun and interesting — but you must know **where** to do it. It's no good to make changes any old place.

Songs are made up of sections, just as paragraphs are made up of sentences. Here's an illustration of the sections in OLD MACDONALD HAD A FARM.

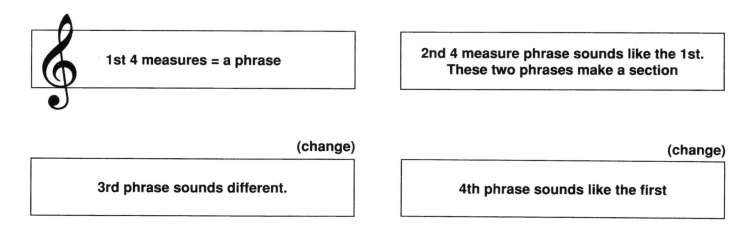

1st 4 measures = a phrase	2nd 4 measure phrase sounds like the 1st. These two phrases make a section
(change)	(change)
3rd phrase sounds different.	4th phrase sounds like the first

The word *change* is used in the music for OLD MACDONALD HAD A FARM to help you know where to make voice or rhythm changes.

Changing Rhythms

You can have a lot of fun by changing rhythms when you play, especially when the time signature is 4/4. Rhythms that fit are ROCK (or 8-BEAT, or POP), SLOW ROCK (or ROCK BALLAD), SWING, DISCO and Latin rhythms such as SALSA, BOSSA NOVA and RHUMBA.

Changing Voices

No matter what the time signature is, you can always change melody voices as you play. Be sure to pick voices that fit the style of the melody. This song, for example, has some shorter notes, so voices that fade away like the piano or vibes work well.

Old MacDonald Had A Farm

Registration 5
Rhythm: Country or Shuffle

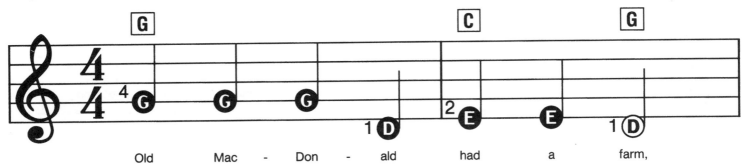

Old Mac - Don - ald had a farm,

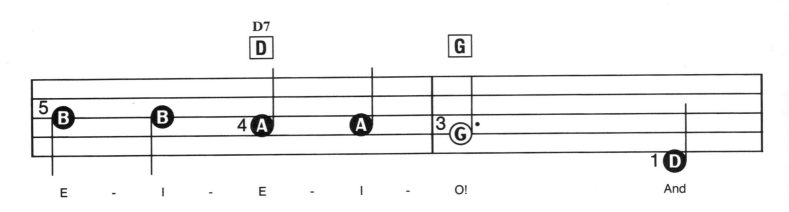

E - I - E - I - O! And

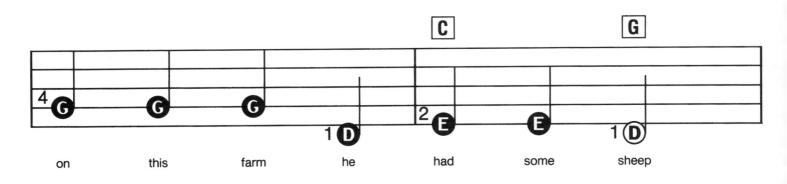

on this farm he had some sheep

Change

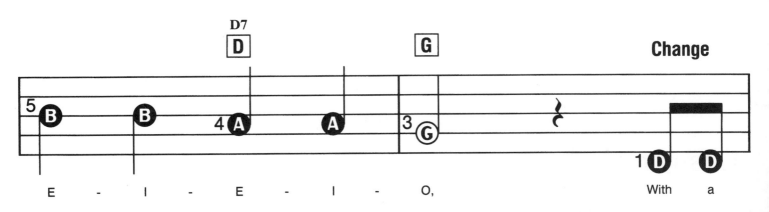

E - I - E - I - O, With a

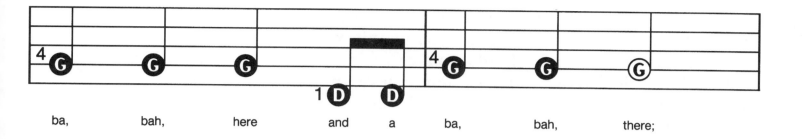

ba,   bah,   here   and   a   ba,   bah,   there;

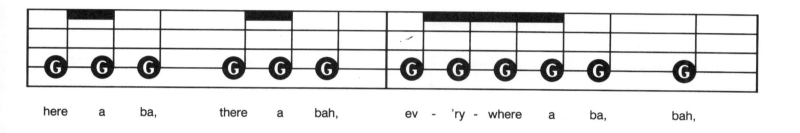

here   a   ba,   there   a   bah,   ev - 'ry - where   a   ba,   bah,

Change

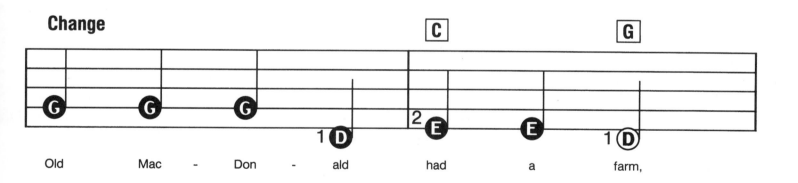

Old   Mac - Don - ald   had   a   farm,

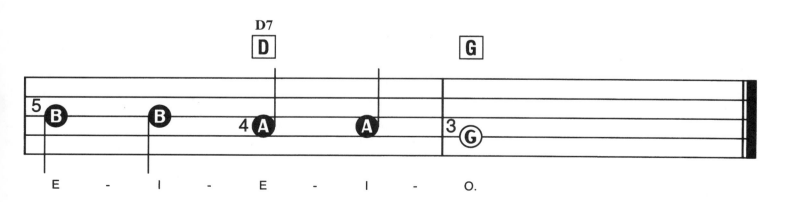

E - I - E - I - O.

Minor Seventh Chords

These are four-note chords that make an interesting sound. The G minor seventh (Gm7) is used as an optional chord in A BICYCLE BUILT FOR TWO. That means it's your choice whether you play it or not, just like the seventh chords you've played before. If you decide not to play a minor seventh chord, ignore the chord above the box and play just the minor chord.

Be sure to check your owner's manual to see how minor seventh chords are formed.

A Bicycle Built For Two

Registration 4
Rhythm: Waltz

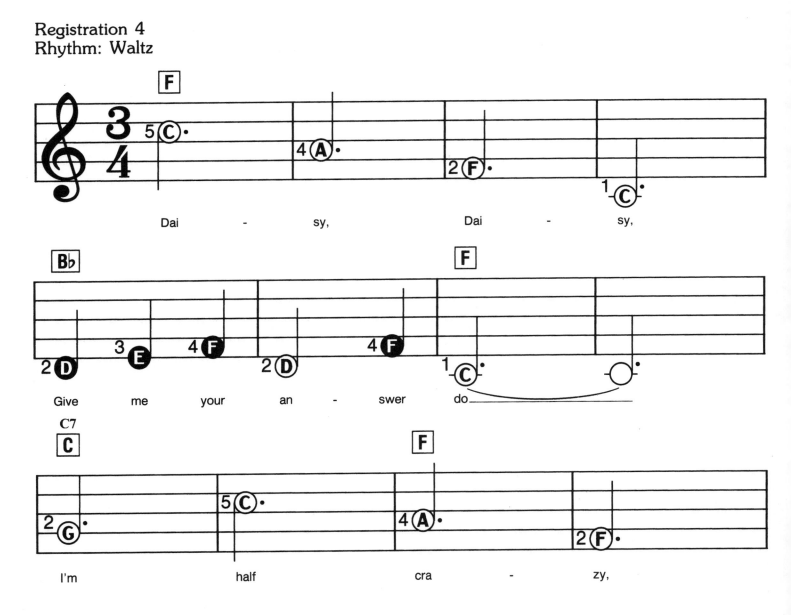

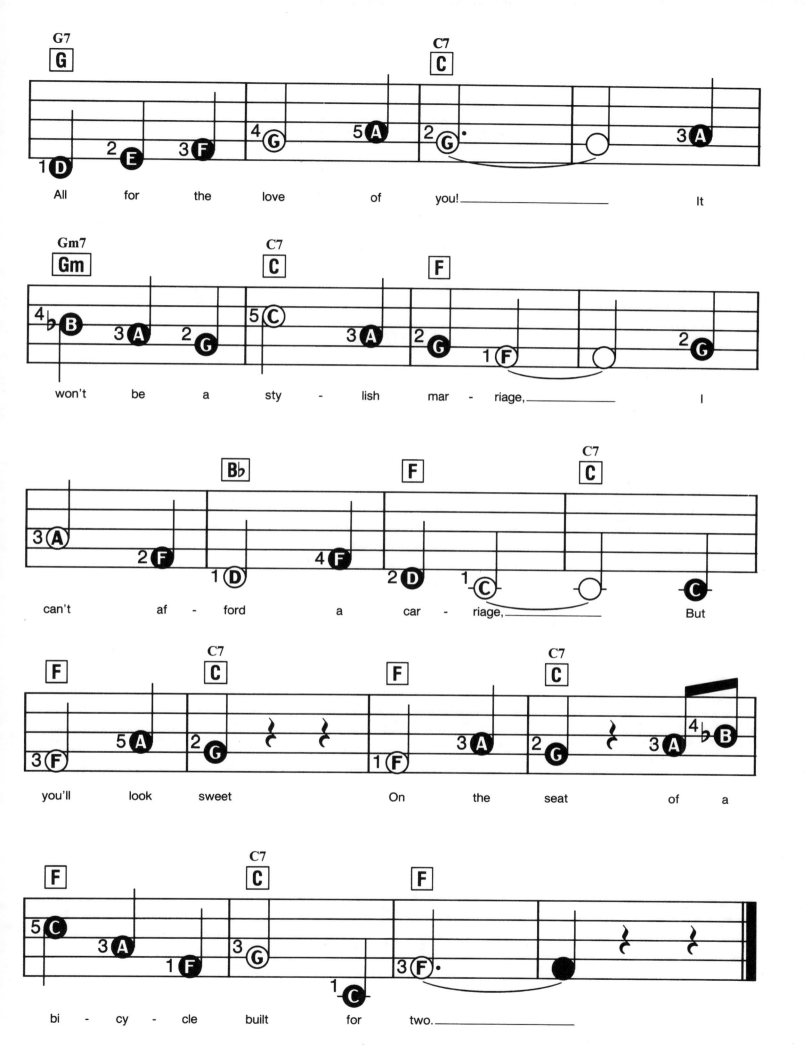

Syncopation

This is pronounced *sink-o-PAY-shun*, and it's very important in music. It can make you want to dance or tap your foot to a popular tune, whether it's a love song or the latest rap record. If you've heard a symphony orchestra, you know the music they play does not make you want to dance. Most of the music a symphony orchestra plays isn't syncopated (SINK-o-pay-ted).

The easiest way to explain syncopation is to say that it happens when a note is played just before you think it will be played. Count out loud as you tap your foot and play this:

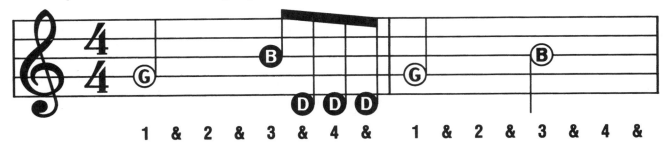

Here is the same thing with the half note changed to a dotted quarter note and the B played early. This is from LA CUCARACHA. Count out loud as you tap your foot and play.

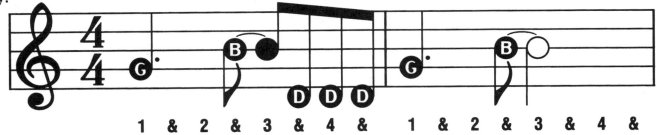

Here are the third and fourth full measures of the song, without syncopation. Count out loud, tap your foot and play.

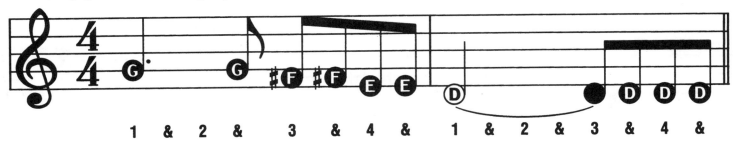

And here it is with syncopation.

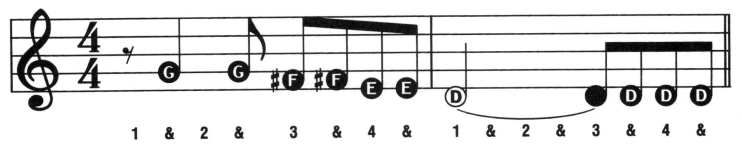

Syncopation makes the music sound "jazzy" and swing.

La Cucaracha

Registration 5
Rhythm: Samba or Latin

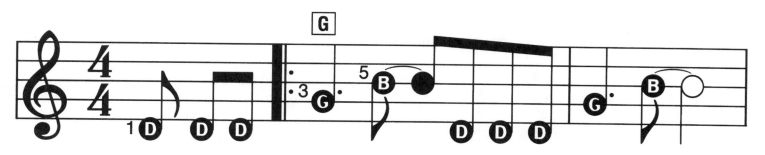

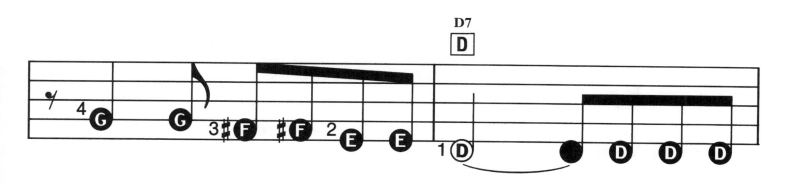

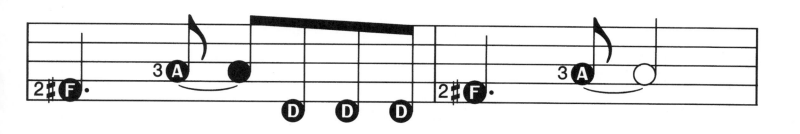

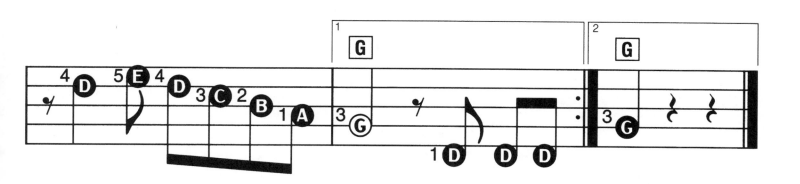

New Time Signature: 6/8

In BOOK 1, you learned that the upper number of a time signature tells you how many beats are in each measure of a song, and that the lower number tells you what kind of note gets one beat.

JACK AND JILL is written in 6/8 time. What does this time signature tell you? It says there are six beats in each measure and that the eighth note gets a beat. Here's how it looks.

The answer to your question is both. An eighth note is a half-beat long — whenever the lower number in the time signature is 4. But in 6/8 time, it gets an entire beat. Not only that, a quarter note gets two beats in 6/8 time. The thing that never changes is that two eighth notes ALWAYS equal one quarter note. Do you get it?

This chart should help you understand.

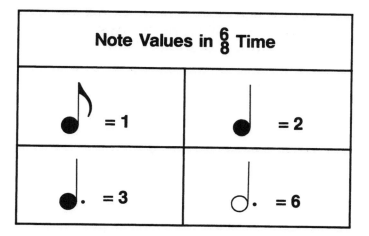

The 6/8 Gallop

When faster songs in 6/8 time, such as JACK AND JILL, are played, the rhythm of the notes might remind you of a horse galloping. Play the examples below to see how this happens. Go slowly and don't use the automatic rhythm.

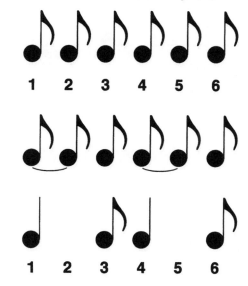

It's the quarter note followed by the eighth note that makes the galloping effect.

Here's the same thing from JACK AND JILL.

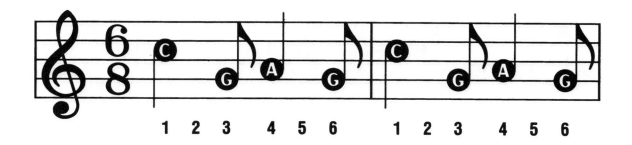

33

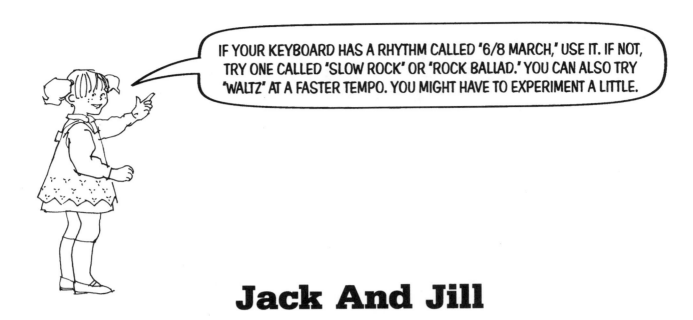

Jack And Jill

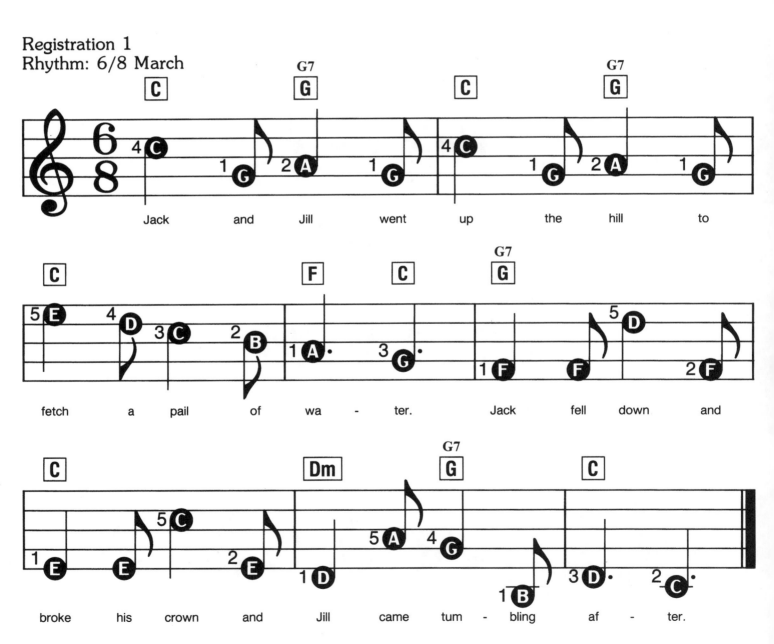

Registration 1
Rhythm: 6/8 March

Minor Key

When you play the next song, GREENSLEEVES, you may notice it has a sort of sad quality to it. This is mostly because the song is written in a minor key. We don't have room in this book to explain all about keys, scales and things like that. We'll simply tell you to look at the second ending, where the song ends. You'll see that the last chord in the song is E minor. If the last chord in a song is a minor chord, it usually tells you that the song is in a minor key — in this case, the key of E minor.

All of the songs you've played up to now have been in major keys. If you look at the last chord in any of them, you'll see a major chord. Major chords have only a letter in the chord symbol, like C, F or others — no M's or 7's.

More About Sharps

In GREENSLEEVES, you will play three new sharp keys. They are C♯, D♯ and high C♯, are shown below along with their position on the keyboard.

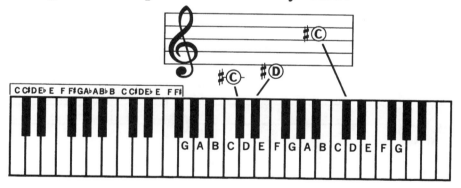

New Chords: B, B7

You will also play two new chords in GREENSLEEVES. They are B and B7 . B is shown in the diagram below. Check your Owner's Manual on how to play a B7 chord.

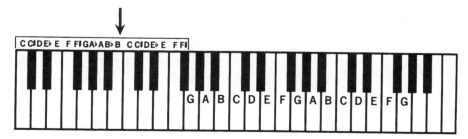

Greensleeves

Registration 1
Rhythm: Waltz

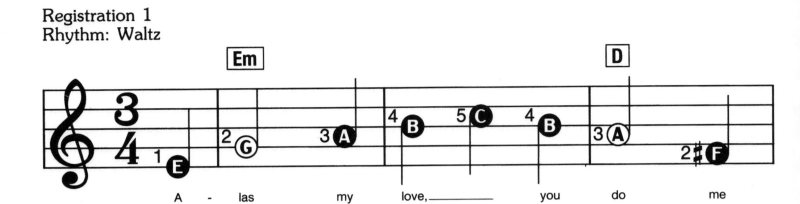

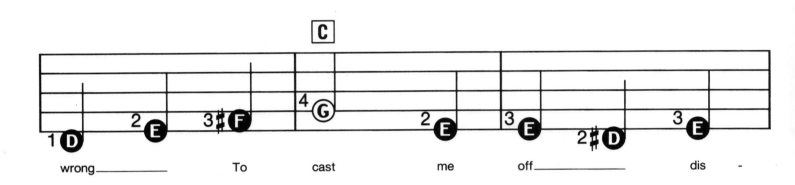

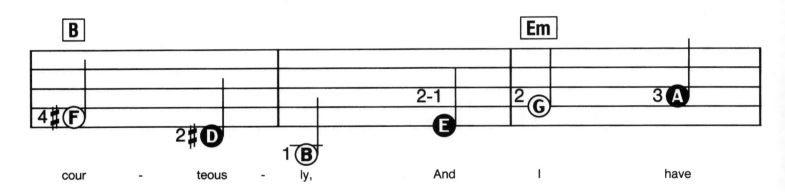

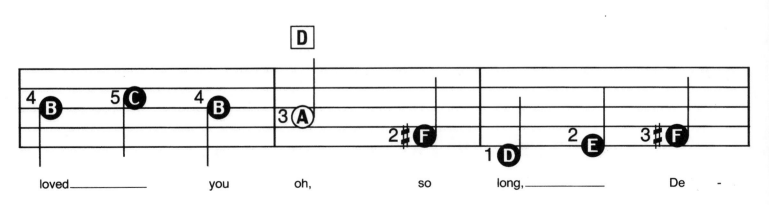

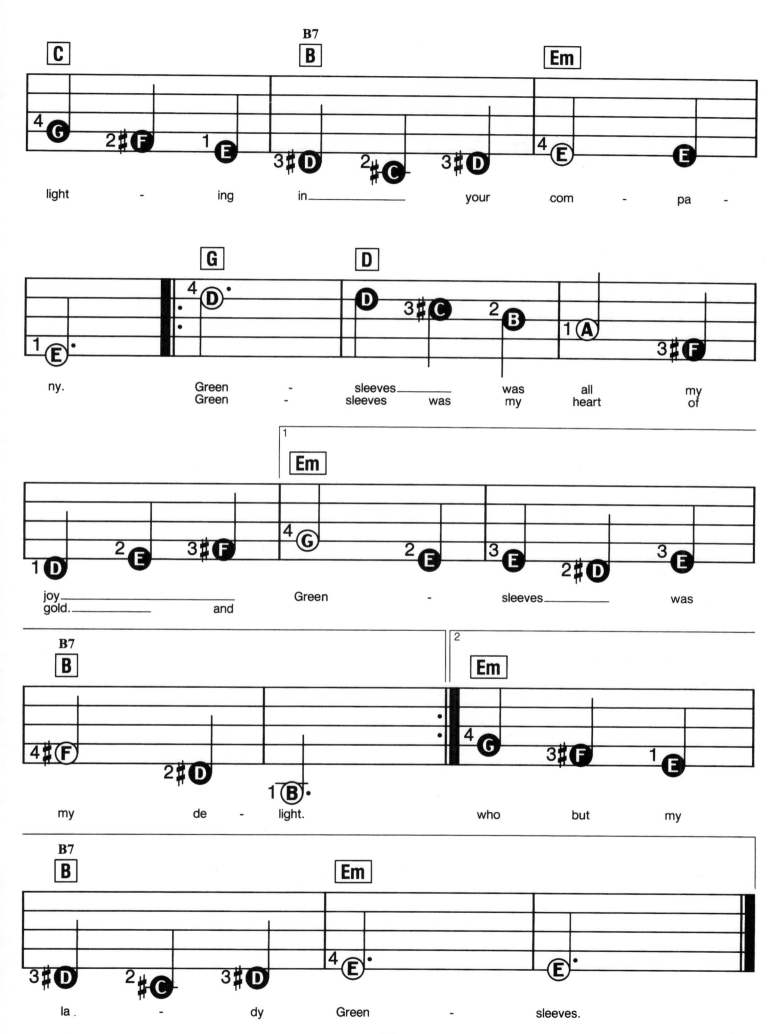

Practice in 6/8 Time

When you play this song, remember the "6/8" gallop.

I've Been Working On The Railroad

Registration 2
Rhythm: 6/8 March

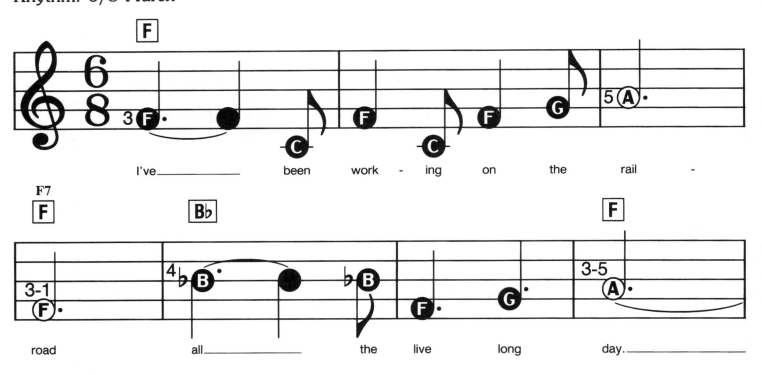

I've ____ been work - ing on the rail -
road all ____ the live long day.

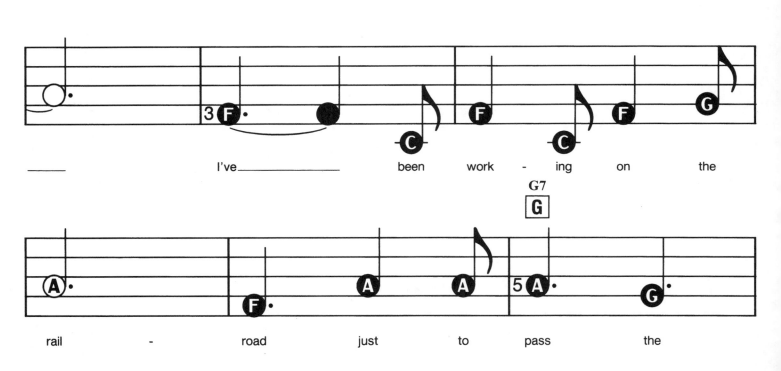

____ I've ____ been work - ing on the
rail - road just to pass the

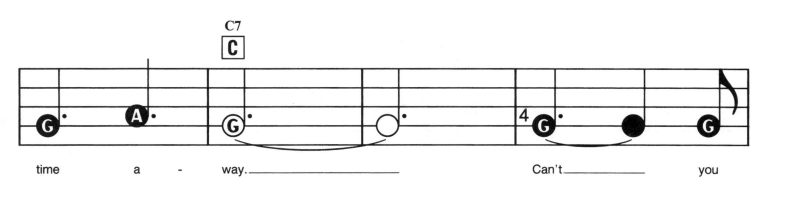

time a - way._____ Can't_____ you

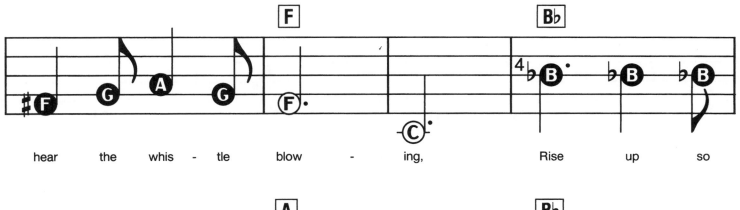

hear the whis - tle blow - ing, Rise up so

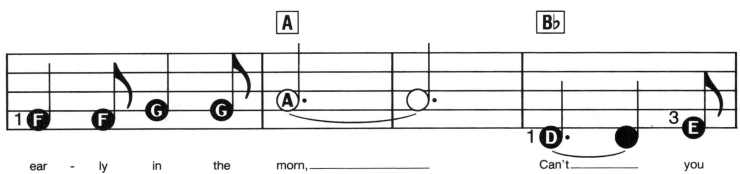

ear - ly in the morn,_____ Can't_____ you

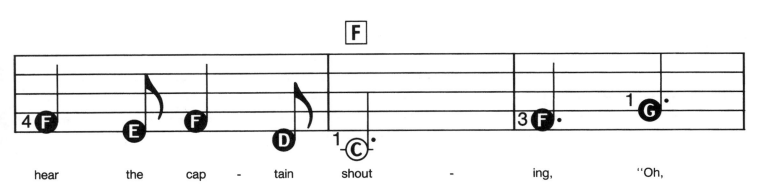

hear the cap - tain shout - ing, "Oh,

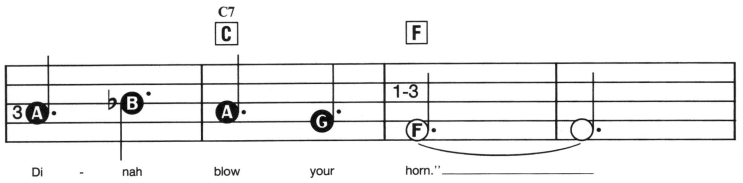

Di - nah blow your horn."_____

Fingering Review

Remember in BOOK 1 when you used a finger crossing to play CAN CAN? Your third finger crossed over your thumb so you didn't run out of fingers. In OLD KING COLE you will also use a finger crossing, but this time it will be a bit different. This time, only your second finger will cross over your thumb as shown below.

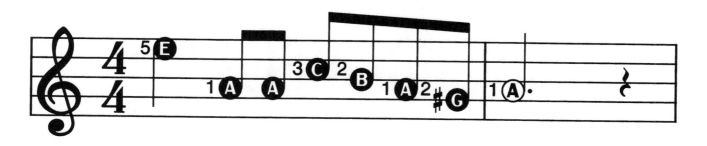

The following exercises will give you a chance to practice little pieces of OLD KING COLE.

Follow the finger numbers very carefully as you play. In the first exercise your second finger crosses over your thumb to play the G♯.

Second Finger Over   **Second Finger Over**

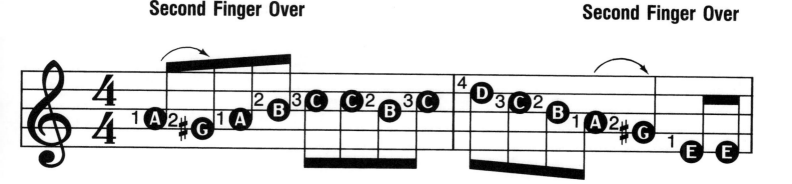

Here, your thumb comes under the second finger to play the A.

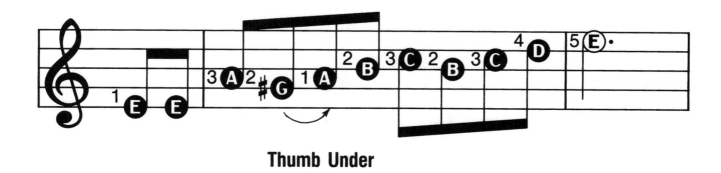

Thumb Under

After practicing these special finger crossings, go on to play OLD KING COLE.

New Notes: G♯, High F

Your next song, OLD KING COLE, uses a new black key, G♯ and high F. Here is what they look like and where they are on the keyboard.

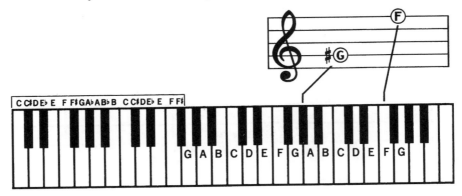

Old King Cole

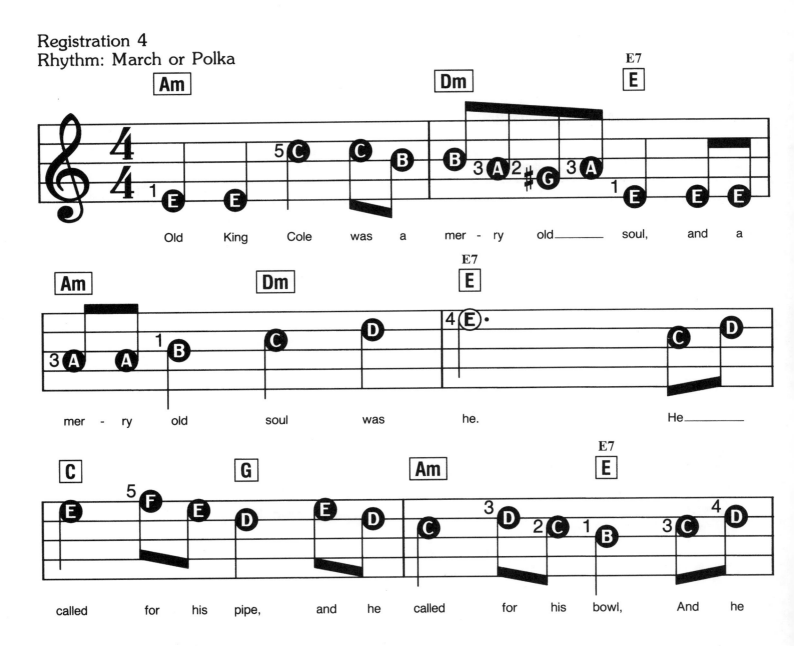

Registration 4
Rhythm: March or Polka

Old King Cole was a mer-ry old_____ soul, and a mer-ry old soul was he. He_____ called for his pipe, and he called for his bowl, And he

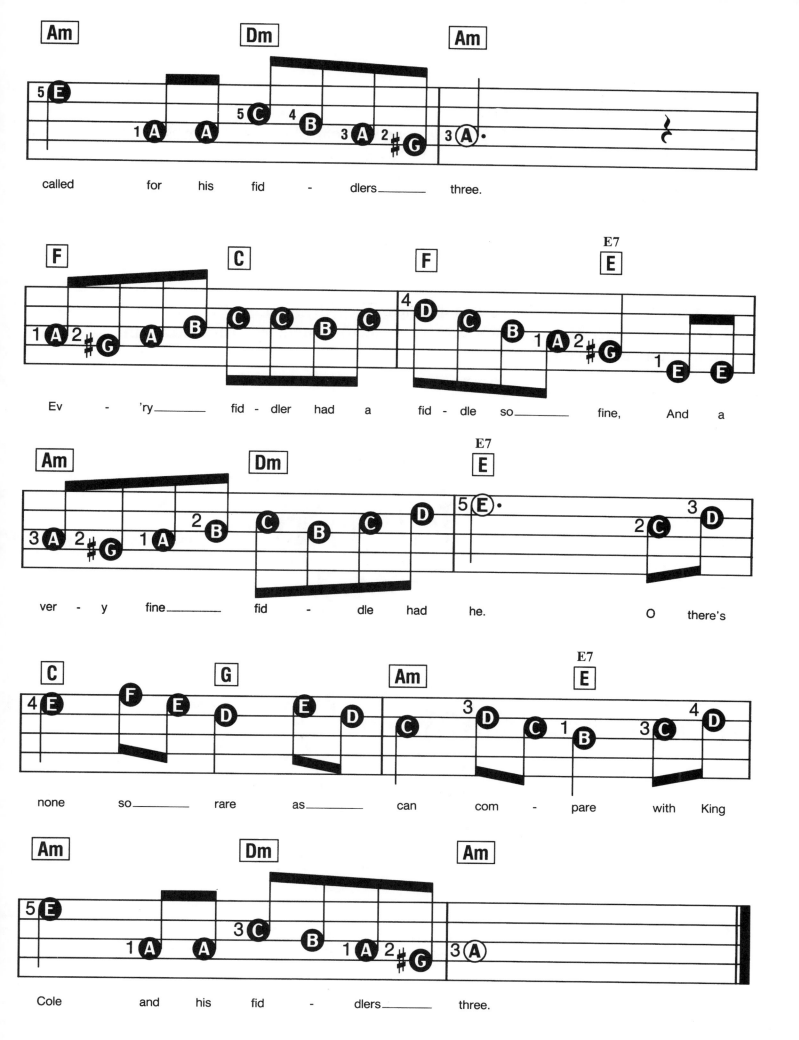

Use Your Headphones

Sometimes you might feel like playing your keyboard but your mom is on the phone or your dad is watching a ball game on TV. No problem! If you have a set of headphones, you can plug them in and your playing won't bother anyone.

If your headphones go with your portable tape player, you might have to get an adapter. Most keyboards need a 1/4" plug. Stores that sell tape players or other electronic stuff usually sell the right type of adapter.

Be careful when you put on the headphones. They'll sound a lot louder than the speaker on your keyboard because they are so close to your ears. Turn down the keyboard volume a bit before you play.

More On Syncopation

DOWN BY THE RIVERSIDE uses syncopation. LA CUCARACHA used syncopation too, but in a little different way. Instead of just one note played "early," like in LA CUCARACHA, two notes in this song are played before you think they would be played. Play and count the example below.

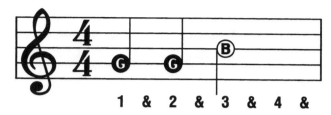

Now play the example below and notice that the second note is played before you expect it. The example on the left is how you can count it out loud. The example on the right is the same rhythm, but is how you will see it in the music.

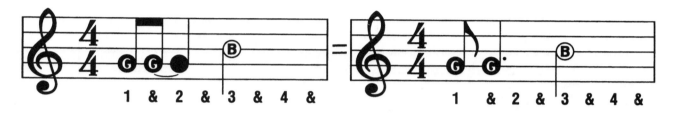

Finally, play the last example and notice the third note comes before the third beat, instead of right on beat three. The example on the right is how you will see it in the music.

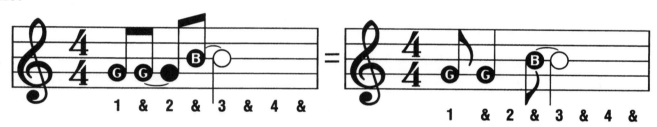

Go on and play DOWN BY THE RIVERSIDE. Notice how the syncopation makes the melody lively and playful.

D.S. al Coda

DOWN BY THE RIVERSIDE also uses a D.S. al Coda sign. Play the song through until the words "D.S. al Coda." Go back to the sign (%) and play until the "To Coda" sign. Jump from the "To Coda" sign to the Coda and play to the end. Here is a map that shows you how it works.

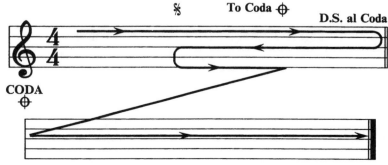

Down By The Riverside

Registration 9
Rhythm: March or Swing

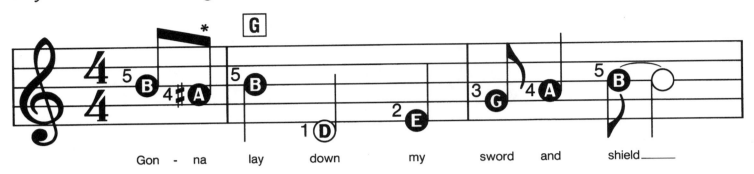

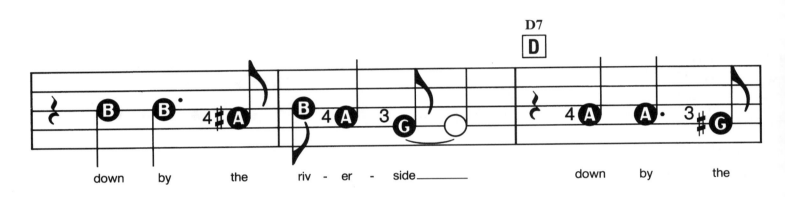

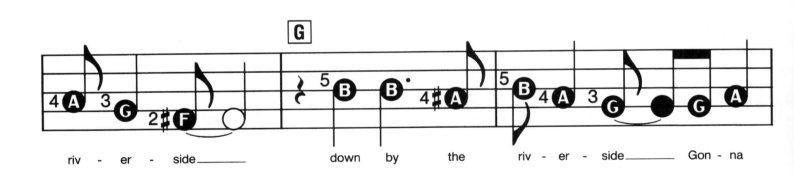

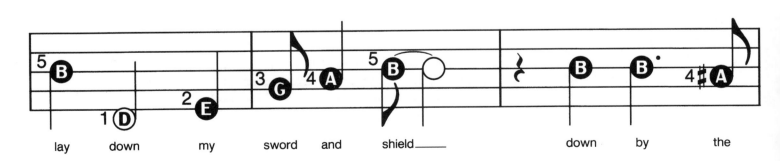

* This is a new note, A-sharp.

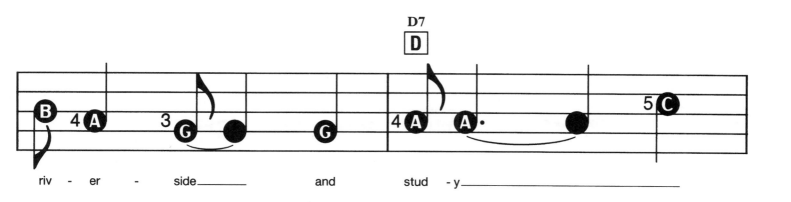

riv - er - side____ and stud -y____

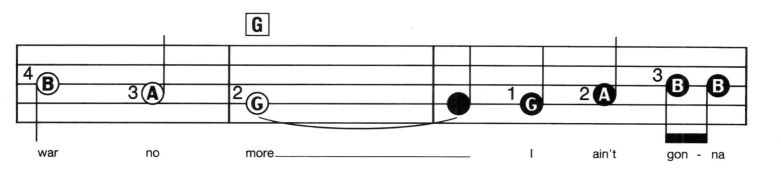

war no more____ I ain't gon - na

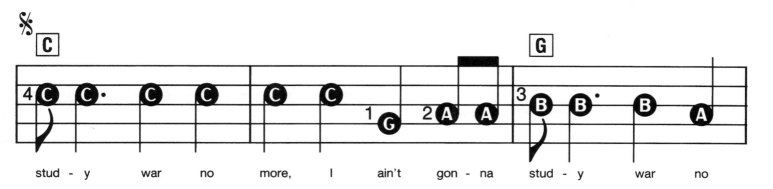

stud - y war no more, I ain't gon - na stud - y war no

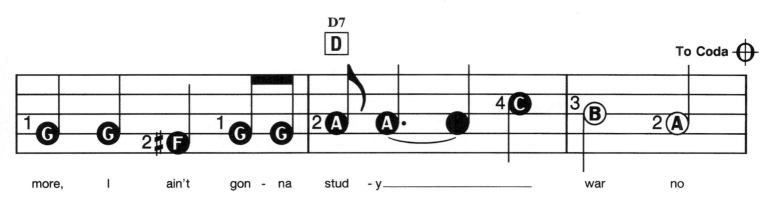

more, I ain't gon - na stud -y____ war no

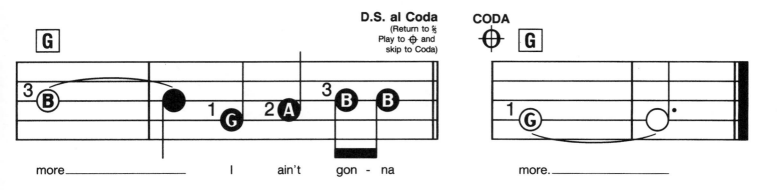

more____ I ain't gon - na   more.____